# THE HEART
# OF THE BUDDHA-DHARMA:
*following the Jodo Shinshu Path*

Kenryu T. Tsuji

First Printing, 2003
ISBN: 1-886439-22-2

Published by
Ekoji Buddhist Temple and
Numata Center for Buddhist Translation and Research
2620 Warring Street
Berkeley, California 94704, USA

Printed in the United States of America

# TABLE OF CONTENTS

*The Dharma is the truth, the Dharma is the law of the universe. The heart of the Buddha-Dharma is the power of infinite wisdom and compassion that has been operating throughout timeless time for the supreme purpose of enlightening all things.*

*In my religious consciousness, this power is personified and called Amida Buddha.*

# FOREWORD

The text for *The Heart of the Buddha-Dharma* was extracted from Dharma messages, pamphlets and temple newsletter columns written by Rev. Kenryu T. Tsuji over a forty-year period. Rev. Tsuji left this treasure chest of material to the Ekoji Buddhist Temple Sangha upon his retirement as resident minister of the Temple in August 1999. Originally intended for the library archives, it was soon realized that by recasting the material in the form of a primer on the Buddha-Dharma, Rev. Tsuji's insight to, and understanding of, the Buddha-Dharma could benefit a wider audience, one beyond the temple doors.

The Sangha of Ekoji Buddhist Temple is indebted to the late Mitsu Yasuda Carl, who as senior editor of the temple newsletter, the *Kalavinka*, compiled and organized the entire set of *Kalavinka* issues since its inception in 1981. This collection served as the source for the section titled "84,000 Thoughts."

We also wish to express our profound appreciation for the generosity and support of the Sangha of the Ekoji Buddhist Temple and its many friends. As this

Temple's Sangha, we were fortunate in knowing Rev. Tsuji and benefiting directly from his many years of service as our resident minister. Further as we are also the beneficiaries of his previous work with the Buddhist Churches of America (BCA), as its first Director of Buddhist Education and then as Bishop of the BCA, we continue to be guided today by his profound vision of what Ekoji should be.

We also appreciate the assistance of the Rev. Gyodo Kono Fund whose board not only helped cultivate the seeds of thought for *The Heart of the Buddha-Dharma*, but also helped with its distribution to the temples and Sanghas of the Buddhist Churches of America, the Buddhist Churches of Canada, and the Hawaii Kyodan.

Finally, though certainly not least, we wish to thank the Bukkyo Dendo Kyokai America, its Director, Mr. Brian Nagata, and Mr. Toshihide Numata and his family. If it were not for the Numata family and Bukkyo Dendo Kyokai, it would not have been possible for Rev. and Mrs. Tsuji to take up their ministry (for they were very much a team) in the Washington, D.C. area. We would not have benefited from our association with them, we would not have the beautiful temple in which Rev. Tsuji labored in his ministry, and we would not have this book that is the product of Rev. Tsuji's forty-year ministry in Canada, the BCA, and at Ekoji.

After his enlightenment some 2,500 years ago, Siddhartha, the historical Buddha, told his followers to go in every direction and to share the Buddha-Dharma "for the benefit of the many, for the welfare of humanity, out of compassion for the world." Over the centuries, our ministers have continued to do that, and Rev. Tsuji is very much a part of that tradition. It is our hope that this book helps carry on Rev. Tsuji's dedicated work in guiding us to understand the Heart of the Buddha-Dharma.

Namo Amida Butsu

Kennon H. Nakamura
*President*

Valorie Lee
*Compiler*

Ekoji Buddhist Temple
Fairfax Station, Virginia
March 2003

# ABOUT THE AUTHOR

Kenryu T. Tsuji was the first Japanese-American Bishop of the Buddhist Churches of America (BCA), a position he held from 1968-1981.

Rev. Tsuji was born in Mission City, British Columbia, Canada on March 14, 1919. He left Canada in 1938 to study Buddhism at Ryukoku University (Kyoto, Japan), receiving his ordination in 1941. Shortly thereafter, however, as rumors of an impending war grew, he was advised to leave and quickly departed for home on one of the last boats out of Japan. Back in Canada, he briefly served at the Vancouver Buddhist Church until, with the outbreak of the Pacific War, he was forcibly relocated to an internment camp in Slocan, British Columbia. At the Slocan Evacuation Camp, he was made principal of the elementary school while also serving as resident minister of the Buddhist Church and it was there that he met his future wife, Sakaye Kawabata, an elementary school teacher. When the war ended, those internees able to find employment were permitted to relocate to the east coast. Rev. Tsuji found work on a mushroom farm in a small town outside Toronto. Within a year, he left to attend the University of Toronto supporting himself and his family with work as a dishwasher and other menial jobs.

In 1946 Rev. Tsuji, along with a handful of devout Buddhist followers from the western Canadian coast, held the first Obon service in Canada; this seminal event led to the formation, in 1947, of the Toronto Buddhist Church. His pioneering efforts would result in the establishment of temples in Hamilton, Ontario and Montreal, Quebec. Rev. Tsuji led the Toronto congregation until 1959, when an invitation came from Bishop Shigefuji of the BCA, to serve as Director of the newly created, Bureau of Buddhist Education. Rev. and Mrs. Tsuji and their children moved to San Francisco, location of the BCA Headquarters. As head of the Education Bureau, Rev. Tsuji developed many programs to promote the Buddha-Dharma, including adult education seminars, the publication of books, pamphlets and ministerial aids, and the establishment of the BCA Buddhist Bookstore. After he was installed as the first western-born Bishop of the BCA in 1968, he translated a broad vision integrating all aspects of the Buddhist tradition into innovative programs and formal study, including the curriculum of the Institute of Buddhist Studies (IBS).

Upon retirement from the BCA in 1981, Rev. Tsuji and Rev. Dr. Yehan Numata, founded Ekoji Buddhist

Temple ("Temple of the Gift of Light") in northern Virginia. Rev. Tsuji and Dr. Numata shared a vision of Ekoji as a venue to minister support for the practice of Shin Buddhism and as a beacon of education and contemplation in Buddhism for denizens of the national capital area. To realize this vision, Rev. Tsuji organized and hosted spring and fall seminars for ministers and lay members on the eastern and midwest states where they would discuss and contemplate the Buddha-Dharma. Notable Buddhist scholars and lecturers were invited to Ekoji as guest speakers while a weekly meditation for adults and monthly services for Japanese speaking members were added to the list of Ekoji programs. In addition to his duties as resident minister at Ekoji, Rev. Tsuji actively participated in interfaith activities, including World Religion Day. He served as president of the World Conference on Religion and Peace from 1983-1989.

To accommodate the growing Ekoji membership as well as to lay the groundwork for the future, a larger temple was built in 1998 close to the first Ekoji Temple site. To meet the needs of smaller-sized Shin Buddhist groups forming in the southeastern states, Rev. Tsuji helped form the Ekoji Buddhist Sangha of Richmond, Virginia and the Augusta Buddhist Sangha in Georgia. Rev. and Mrs. Tsuji devoted much of their spare time and energy to these groups by regular visits to the temples where they would cultivate growth and encourage the membership. Recognizing the importance of out-reach in fostering knowledge of the Buddha-Dharma, Rev. Tsuji traveled to various states to lecture on Buddhism.

After an extraordinary 57 years of service in the Buddhist ministry, Rev. Kenryu T. Tsuji retired in 1999. He and Mrs. Tsuji currently reside in Foster City, California.

# RECOLLECTIONS, I

I came to know Rev. and Mrs. Tsuji when they lived at the Huron Street church location in 1947 which became the first Toronto Buddhist Church.

Soon after the establishment of the Toronto Buddhist Church, Rev. Tsuji began working on the formation of a Nisei Buddhist group in Hamilton and in Montreal, which later became churches.

Major services and large meetings were held at the Legion Hall and later as the numbers of Dharma school students grew, it was also held at the Hall.

About this time, Mr. Yehan Numata met Rev. Tsuji. He was very much impressed with the energetic activities and the foresight of Rev. Tsuji which I believe led to the selection of Rev. Tsuji to eventually organize and lead the Washington DC Ekoji congregation.

Rev. Tsuji started a study class and named it the Asoka Society. It was for members interested in the Buddhist philosophy and for discussions. At one of these gatherings, the subject of building a new church was mentioned. One of the prominent members of the group suggested that when you open the church door, you are inviting the public; therefore you must be ready to meet and be able to answer their questions. It will be a good idea to have leaflets and pamphlets ready for distribution.

With the completion of the new church, we began to see leaflets and pamphlets by Rev. Tsuji. At the Sunday morning services, brief notes on the sermon of the week before began to appear on the front information table. These publications were introduced to the Buddhist Churches of America (BCA) when Rev. Tsuji became the Director of Buddhist Education.

Another innovative idea originated by Rev. Tsuji was the initiation of an annual special study class for the new incoming church cabinet members so that they would not be embarrassed by the questions asked by visitors.

I believe the late Bishop Enryo Shigefuji, who was the overseer of all Canadian churches at the time, recognized the leadership quality, patience and determination to bring the job to completion in Rev. Tsuji when he appointed him as Director of the new Bureau of Buddhist Education. Later it opened the path in time for him to become the Bishop of BCA and then on to be the minister for the Washington DC Ekoji Temple.

Rev. Tsuji completed three terms (13 years) as Bishop of the BCA. He introduced a program in 1975 called the New Horizon Project for members to go out to new communities and institutions to spread the Buddha-Dharma. He had done it many times over in Canada then and now in the United States.

Rev. Tsuji has been very generous in putting his special talents to use in every possible way so the Nembutsu can be shared with many.

In Gassho,


Ensei H. Nekoda,
*BCA Minister Emeritus*

November 2002

# RECOLLECTIONS, II

It was sixty-three years ago, on a warm spring day in Kyoto, Japan, when a dashing young man in a tan suit, unlike most students at Ryukoku University, rambled down a street between the main campus and the seminary division. After being introduced, I would learn that this young man was Takashi Tsuji from Canada. We became schoolmates in the seminary division in 1939.

Ministerial scholarship students from the continental U.S. and Canada commuted from "Wakoryo," a dormitory for students attending Ryukoku University, and the dorm's overseer was the Dean of the University, Rev. Kenju Masuyama. Amongst these students were persons who responded to nicknames such as "Mac, Bori, Oxy, Tak" and so on and would later become Reverends Kumata, Tsunoda, Masunaga and Tsuji.

Reverend Tsuji's inherent talent and inclination were discovered by Rev. Nishu Utsuki who headed the Hongwanji Translation Department. After school hours, Rev. Tsuji would spend most of his time assisting Rev. Utsuki's translation work, and his accomplishments are evident today.

Tsuji Sensei's motivational leadership can be seen in his work with the International Buddhist Sunday School (IBSS). At that time, Kyoto attracted many Nisei students from Hawaii, Canada and the continental United States. This group met monthly in the auditorium of the new Ryukoku University Library. The order and format of the church services we witness in today's churches in Hawaii, the continental U.S. and Canada are patterned after the IBSS service order, which acted as experimental grounds for "western" churches.

I am familiar with Reverend Tsuji's exploits until July of 1941, when I suddenly departed back for California. It wasn't until later that I would learn that sensei also left Japan and was able to safely return to Canada before the outbreak of World War II.

During my association at Yale University, the Canadian Nikkeis were forced into incarceration, as were all Japanese Americans on the west coast. Several thousand Canadian Nikkei eventually relocated to eastern Canada, and among them was Rev. Tsuji. He found employment on a mushroom farm.

Despite these hard times, sensei had a vision to initiate a movement to establish a center to propagate Shinshu teachings in Canada. Through his tireless efforts, and especially with the support of his lovely wife, Sakaye, there are today two churches in Ontario

Province and one in Quebec which were started by Rev. Tsuji. These are truly a tribute to Rev. Tsuji's charismatic leadership.

There is a distinctive difference in the Buddhist Churches of America, post- and prior-Tsuji, especially in the area of Buddhist education.

One of Rev. Tsuji's outstanding talents is his oratorical skill, something that was quite evident from his Kyoto days and throughout his BCA career.

Some of his salient characteristics can be summed up with his warm and attentive mien. To be a tremendous leader required extensive know-how and he spared no time in acquiring this knowledge.

He had five daughters and each of their children is a tribute to Tak and Sakaye's upbringing. My wife and I also had five children, not that there was any imitation involved, it was just coincidence.

I feel so privileged to be called his friend, in spite of my inferior quality. We all miss his leadership today, but it is up to the present generation to excel in every way to keep this Nembutsu movement alive and well. Gassho.

Rev. Newton Ishiura
*BCA Minister Emeritus*

December 2002

# RECOLLECTIONS, III

My father had many accomplishments in the larger community but he was also a great dad to the five of us girls – his gifts to us, his great sense of humor, his dedication to accomplishing his goals, his openness and friendliness to everyone.

My dad had a great sense of humor and would often weave corny or even slightly risqué jokes into his sermon. When he was writing a sermon, he would often work late into the night, with books open around him, not just Buddhist texts but also *Bartlett's Familiar Quotations, Two Thousand Jokes for All Occasions*, and books on speaking and writing. He believed writing a good sermon was a craft and paid attention to how long he could hold a congregation's attention, how many ways he could illustrate his main theme, and how he delivered his message.

Even though my father was always a very busy man, my mom and he would take us and our spaniel, Lady Nirvana, camping every summer, and we had many adventures like dad trying to teach us how to pitch a tent. Lots of squeals, not much construction.

One night we sat in a small tent in the pouring rain with dad telling us not to touch the ceiling because it would create a leak. We immediately reached up and created four leaks. These are things kids just have to do. My dad patiently went outside with waxed paper to cover the leaks and returned moments later truly drenched.

My father used to talk to us children about the "three I's - intelligence, integrity, and initiative." Although we groaned when he would remind us that we had neglected to use one or more of these traits, I realize now this is how my dad lived his life.

My father traveled a lot and he would always bring home a souvenir, four, and then five for each of us, of exactly the same thing, a key chain or beads, and once a Seiko watch (which I still have and which still works). It came to be a family joke - five of these cost a hundred dollars or more!

All through our childhood, I remember my father bringing home visitors to spend the night, often with no notice. I think traveling monks and students would look up "Buddhist" in the white pages and then call Buddhist Churches of America looking for a place to stay and, sure enough, my dad would accommodate them. They would sleep on the foldout couch in our tiny living room, sometimes accompanied by our dog, Ginger. We sent many Chinese, Japanese, and Indian monks on their way with blond dog hair clinging to their robes.

So many of the wonderful traits my father exemplified are gone now, dimmed by Alzheimer's. However, his sense of humor still surfaces occasionally, as corny as ever. My dad's many selfless gifts to us all live on in our memories and in what we do in turn to give to others.

Liz Wadleigh
January 2003

# THE HEART

# OF THE BUDDHA-DHARMA

# I

# The Many Buddhas

## The Historical Buddha

Amid the vernal splendor of Lumbini Garden, Gautama, the Buddha, was born in 566 B.C., as son of a wealthy and powerful king, Suddhodana, the ruler of the Sakya clan, at Kapilavastu in the modern state of Nepal. The Buddha was given the name Siddhartha, which means, "He who has attained his aim."

Rejoicing over the birth of his heir, King Suddhodana made elaborate arrangements to see that nothing was lacking in the life of the prince. For his mental and physical education, sages, soldiers and athletes from all parts of the country were summoned to the castle. Whether it was knowledge requiring the highest of intellect or games taxing the utmost of his physical prowess, the young prince showed remarkable skill of mastery. At nineteen, he was married to Princess Yashodara who bore him a son, Rahula. The royal couple lived amidst inconceivable luxury.

In spite of this unsurpassed beauty and comfort that surrounded the prince at all times, Siddhartha felt deep despair. He wanted to go out to seek the Light of Truth. The faint stirring in his heart steadily grew stronger until at last he could not restrain himself from cutting the fetters that bound him to this existence. Leaving his sleeping wife and son, he went forth into the still Indian night with great resolve to find salvation for himself and his fellow men. He was twenty-nine years of age.

For six years he mingled with ascetics and hermits practicing the difficult system of salvation they taught and subjecting his body to the severest of disciplines, but he realized that the extremes of asceticism, like luxury, led one nowhere. The truest path to Enlightenment, he found, lay in patient and systematic examination of all aspects of life, and discovering the solution to its sufferings.

As he quietly meditated under the Bodhi Tree, there developed in him a deep spiritual insight into the nature of existence. When the day ended and the first stars showed their lights in the sky above, Gautama attained Enlightenment, the highest wisdom man has yet reached. One by one the heavy doubts of life and death, of sorrow — its cause and cure— vanished; the great mystery finally had been solved. He became Buddha, the Fully Enlightened One.

He spent the remaining forty-five years of his life in a labor of love and compassion, and his Teachings spread the whole breadth and length of the country. He passed away at the age of eighty, leaving the following message to his sorrowful disciples: "The Dharma which I have given you shall be your Teacher, when I am gone."

So great has been the influence of this Dharma that today it is estimated one-third of humanity pays homage to his Noble Teachings.

# Infinite Buddha

When the Buddha reached eighty years of age, he began to feel the fatigue of a lifetime of spreading the Dharma. At thirty-five, he had attained Enlightenment and for the following forty-five years, he wandered on foot the whole breadth of northern India teaching the Way of Wisdom and Compassion. When he finally felt he could no longer continue his mission, he asked his disciples to accompany him on his last visit to Vaisali, a city he loved, a city of beautiful towers and palaces, of green meadows and sparkling rivers. The Buddha however, could not reach Vaisali and had to stop to rest in Kusinagara. There, in Kusinagara, he passed away quietly between two sal trees.

As he laid down between the trees, his disciples gathered around him, knowing that the Buddha's end was near. To his disciples the Buddha said,

*"My disciples, my last moment has come, but do not forget that death is only the passing of the physical body... the true Buddha is not a human body, it is Enlightenment. A human body must die, but the wisdom of Enlightenment will exist forever in the truth of the*

*Dharma and in the practice of the Dharma..."*

And then he said,

*"Make of yourself a light. Rely upon yourself; do not depend on anyone else."*

In these immortal words, the Buddha taught us that there was something greater than the physical body. He was pointing to the power of Enlightenment, a power that all beings possess. Too often attached to the visible body, we forget the invisible, potential power the human body possesses — to enlighten ourselves and to help others become enlightened. This is the true energy of human life that never perishes. The physical body dies but this energy never dies. *Make of yourself a light.* These are powerful words.

We must search for the inner light, which is the infinite Buddha within. Nobody can find the Buddha for us. Each person must find the Buddha within him or herself. And when we find the Buddha, we realize that it was this Buddha — the great power of Wisdom and Compassion — that has been operating within us throughout timeless time.

# Amida Buddha

In the Jodo Shinshu school of Buddhism, Amida Buddha symbolizes the timeless, unending  power of wisdom and compassion operating throughout the universe. *Amida* stands for *Amitabha* and *Amitayus*. *Amitabha* is Infinite Light and *Amitayus* is Infinite Life. Light is the symbol of Supreme Wisdom and Life is the symbol of Infinite Compassion. Infinite here means "all embracing."

By the very nature of the power of wisdom and compassion, Amida Buddha completes the enlightenment of sentient beings. Why is it that we are incapable of completing our own enlightenment? — essentially because we are tainted by egocentricity and selfishness. Therefore, one must come to a realization of their existential limitations and awaken to the wisdom and compassion of Amida Buddha.

With this religious insight comes a deeper dimension of existence. From the lower level of the small individual self of everyday life consciousness, we rise to a higher level of consciousness to become fully awakened to the universal consciousness of Amida

Buddha. This faith in Amida, this inner light of wisdom, becomes a dynamic force within our lives.

# II

# Fundamental Teachings

## The Buddha-Dharma

The correct term for Buddhism is Buddha-Dharma. Buddha-Dharma has two definitions: the teaching of the Buddha and the teaching that guides all beings to Buddhahood. The latter points to the true purpose of the Buddha-Dharma: the ultimate goal for humanity is to attain Buddhahood, or to become enlightened.

Buddhism is a religion of personal realization and awakening and so is often compared to a mirror in which one reflects their thinking, action and words.

Unless he looks in the mirror, no man will really see himself; even a little smear of dirt on his face cannot be perceived without the aid of the mirror. And all the more imperceptible are his thoughts, actions and words without means for evaluation and reflection.

In an everyday life beset with sufferings — birth, old age, sickness, death, and all the other complications and frustrations felt by everyone — Buddhism gives us an insight into our lives, and teaches us not to flee, but to understand. Thus even in the midst of suffering, the Buddhist is able to appreciate life. The Buddha-Dharma guides us by enabling us to understand our true nature, and thus we can cultivate and improve our self through discipline.

Buddhism is a religion of wisdom and compassion; it teaches that true wisdom is always accompanied by compassion and compassion is always founded on wisdom. The message of Buddha was that we have moved within the power of wisdom and compassion for too long — in ignorance. The supreme task of life is the realization of this great power of wisdom and compassion within: to understand this innate potential energy and to work for its complete fulfillment for our own Enlightenment as well as for the Enlightenment of others.

# Buddha-Nature

Buddha-nature is the innate capacity to look upon all beings with great compassion. Every human being possesses this potentiality. Buddha-nature is the very basis of human dignity and the spiritual foundation of enlightened human relationships. The spirituality of man is greater than his physical or intellectual being and it is this spirituality, his Buddha-nature, which, when cultivated to its highest state, makes man a Buddha — perfect in Wisdom and perfect in Compassion. The ultimate message of the Buddha was, "Awaken the Buddha-nature in yourself." It is this message that we must clearly hear.

Buddha-nature is not restricted solely to human beings. The fundamental Dharma teaches us that even "the mountains, rivers, trees, grass and all possess Buddha-nature." This means not only human beings but all sentient beings, all things in the universe, possess the capacity to become a Buddha. Once a scientist asked me, "How can a rock become a Buddha?" I replied, "When you have become a Buddha."

# Four Noble Truths

The essence of Buddhism can be summed up in the Fourfold Noble Truths. In the doctrine of the Four Noble Truths, the Buddha gave a true description of life and expressed a true ideal for all men.

The words of the Buddha's first sermon, below in italics, are from the *Majjhima-Nikaya*; the explanatory text following is from the publication, *The Teaching of Buddha* [Bukkyo Dendo Kyokai: Japan]:

**The Four Noble Truths:**

I. Truth of Suffering

*This, O Bhikkus is the Noble Truth of Suffering: birth is suffering, decay is suffering; illness is suffering, death is suffering. Presence of objects we hate is suffering; separation from objects we love is suffering, not to obtain what we desire is suffering.*

The world is full of suffering. Because life is imperfect, there is always suffering, friction, and disharmony. Birth is suffering, decrepitude is suffering, so are sickness and death suffering. To face a man of hatred is suffering, to be separated from a beloved one is suffering, or to be vainly struggling to satisfy one's needs. In fact, life that is not free from desire and passion is always involved with suffering. This is called the Truth of Suffering.

## II.  Truth of the Cause of Suffering

*This, O Bhikkus, is the Noble Truth of the Cause of Suffering: thirst that leads to Rebirth, accompanied by pleasure and lust, finding its delight here and there... thirst for pleasure, thirst for existence, thirst for prosperity.*

The cause of human suffering is undoubtedly found in the thirsts of the physical organism and in the illusions of worldly passion. If these thirsts and illusions are traced to their source, they are found to be rooted in the intense desires of physical instincts. Thus desire, having a strong will to live at its core, goes after what is perceived as being desirable. Sometimes desire even turns towards death. This is called the Truth of the Cause of Suffering.

We suffer because through ignorance we do not see things in their true light.  For example, we consider impermanent things as permanent and become attached to them. When we lose them, we are deeply hurt. To regard impermanence as impermanence is truth.

III. Truth of the Cessation of Suffering

*This, O Bhikkus, is the Noble Truth of the Cessation of Suffering; it is the complete cessation of this thirst — a cessation which consists in the absence of every passion with the abandoning of this thirst, with the doing away with it, with the deliverance from it, with the destruction of desire.*

If desire, which lies at the root of all human passion, can be removed, then passion will die out and all human suffering will end. This is called the Truth of the Ending of Suffering.

The causes of suffering can be extinguished and a perfect state can be established. This perfect state is called by such terms as Nirvana, Enlightenment, Pure Land, and Buddhahood.

IV. Truth of the Path to the Cessation of Suffering

*This, O Bhikkus, is the Noble Truth of the Path which leads to the cessation of suffering: that holy Eightfold Path, that is to say, Right Views, Right Aspirations, Right Speech, Right Conduct, Right Livelihood, Right Effort, Right Mindfulness, Right Meditation.*

In order to enter into a condition where there is no desire and no suffering, one must follow the Noble Eightfold Path:

*Right Views*

To keep ourselves free from prejudice, superstition, and delusion, and to see the true nature of life.

*Right Thoughts*

To turn away from the evils of this world and to direct our minds toward righteousness.

*Right Speech*

To refrain from pointless and harmful talk, and to speak kindly and courteously to all.

*Right Conduct*

To see that our deeds are peaceful, benevolent, compassionate, and pure; to live the Teaching of the Buddha daily.

*Right Livelihood*

To earn our living in such a way as to entail no evil consequences.

*Right Effort*

To direct our efforts incessantly to the overcoming of ignorance and selfish desires.

*Right Mindfulness*

To cherish good and pure thoughts; for all that we say

and do arises from our thoughts.

*Right Meditation*

To concentrate our will on the Buddha, His Life and His Teaching.

# The Nature of Existence

The following are summarized explanations for the Sanskrit terms: *anitya* (impermanence), *duhkha* (suffering) and *anatman* (egolessness).

a) *Anitya* (impermanence) — This is a Sanskrit word meaning that nothing in this world is permanent. What we perceive as solid and unchanging is actually in a state of constant flux; the flowers that bloom today will wither tomorrow. Impermanence is a law of the universe from which nothing can escape, from the mightiest of astronomical systems to the microscopic forms of life.

b) *Duhkha* (suffering) — This word is rendered into English as suffering, sorrow, and dissatisfaction. The first Noble Truth can be summed up in this one word. The cause of *Duhkha* as can be seen in the Second Noble Truth is desire or the clinging to pleasure, existence and prosperity. By the complete eradication of desire by man's own conscious efforts, the Buddha taught that man can attain the realm of absolute Peace and Bliss, Nirvana. The Buddha taught the existence of suffering but also taught the way of deliverance from suffering. He not only diagnosed the sickness but he prescribed a practical cure — the faithful following of the Eightfold Path. "This above all do I teach," He said, "Suffering and the Deliverance from Suffering."

c) *Anatman* (egolessness) — This doctrine states that there is no permanent entity in man that separates him from others, the ego, self or soul. The self or the "I" is made up of a number of attachment groups such as body, sensation, perception, will, and consciousness. The Buddha did not teach the existence of an individual soul that exists apart from the body — and differentiates each one from his neighbor. The "soul" in Buddhism is not an individual, human, animate existence, but is the "spark" of the "Universal Flame," which unifies all animate and inanimate objects. This is the philosophic basis of the Buddhist doctrine of the Oneness of Life.

# Nirvana

Nirvana is the important teaching of the Buddha Dharma. It is the final goal of Buddhist aspiration and practice in which blind passions are extinguished and the highest wisdom is attained. Nirvana literally means extinction: it is the extinction of self-attachment, the "grasping nature" in human existence and the selfish desire which accompanies it.

For all living things, especially human beings, working for self-interest is of paramount concern. In many respects, it is unavoidable. But to become truly humane requires that we rise above our self-attachments, the "little self," and work for the realization of the true universal self, the "Greater Self." When this grasping, the root cause of all delusion, is extinguished completely, the true universal self is realized. This is the Buddha in Nirvana.

# Enlightenment

Enlightenment is the ultimate fulfillment of the human being: the achievement of perfect Wisdom, the perfection of the intellect; and Compassion, the perfect purification of the emotions. The supreme purpose of Buddhism is to turn illusion into Enlightenment.

It is a common belief that Enlightenment occurs suddenly and that it is the single great religious experience in life, but Enlightenment is a growing experience that never stops. Each day we experience the joys and sadness of life, and with each living experience we come to a deeper understanding of the totality of life — its beauty and ugliness, success and failures, victories and defeats, birth and death. Every activity of life has absolute meaning, for every motion, however significant, is the Enlightenment experience.

Enlightenment is found in the earthly realms of suffering, hunger, instinct, conflict, human frailties and pleasure. For the spiritually awakened person, Enlightenment is here and now, amidst the trials and tribulations of human existence. So it was with the Buddha, Shinran Shonin and all the other great religious leaders.

When Prince Siddhartha Gautama set out on his long search for Enlightenment it was surely to attain Enlightenment for himself so that he would find deliverance from the suffering of life. However, once he had attained Enlightenment and became a Buddha, he could not just sit in meditation enjoying his ultimate religious experience. The very nature of his Buddhahood moved him deeply, and immediately, to enlighten others.

The Buddha said:

*Enlightenment has no definite form or nature by which it can manifest itself; so in Enlightenment itself, there is nothing to be enlightened.*

*Enlightenment exists solely because of delusion and ignorance; if they disappear, so will Enlightenment. And the opposite is true also; delusion and ignorance exist because of Enlightenment; when Enlightenment ceases, ignorance and delusion will cease also...*

*Therefore be on guard against thinking of Enlightenment as a "thing" to be grasped, lest it, too, should become an obstruction. When the mind that was in darkness becomes enlightened, it disappears, and with its passing, the thing which we call Enlightenment also disappears.*

# Interdependence

When the Buddha sat under the Bodhi tree and contemplated on life and the world, he came to the
supreme Enlightenment that everything in the universe was interdependent, nothing can stand alone.
From this conception of the universe, it follows that the
self, as an integral part of the universe, exists in an
interdependent relationship with this universe. The air
we breathe, the food we eat, our inherited political
ideas and systems, cultural values or religious teachings make up the "I". Man leans on others for existence,
whether those others are objects, ideals, or fellow
beings; wise indeed were the masters of China when
they composed the character for man as one line lean-
ing against another. The knowing person understands
that he or she is inextricably interrelated to everything
in the world.

With insight it will also be seen that there are
causes and conditions accounting for the existence of
everything. For example, a seed will not grow if left on
a dry concrete sidewalk. It must be planted in fertile
soil; rain and sun must nourish it. All these helping

causes or conditions determine the growth and the final blossom of the seed.

In the sutras, or sacred writings, it states:

*Rain falls, winds blow, plants bloom, leaves mature and are blown away; these phenomena are all interrelated with causes and conditions, are brought about by them and disappear as the causes and conditions change.*

*One is born through the conditions of parentage; his body is nourished by food, his spirit is nurtured by teaching and experience. As a net is made up by a series of ties, so everything in this world is connected by a series of ties. If anyone thinks that the mesh of a net is an independent, isolated thing, he is mistaken.*

*It is the everlasting and unchanging rule of this world that everything is created by a series of causes and conditions and everything disappears by the same rule; everything changes, nothing remains the same.*

# III

## Jodo Shinshu,
## A Brief Introduction

### Jodo Shinshu

Jodo Shinshu ("True Pure Land Religion")[1] was founded by Shinran Shonin (1173-1262).[2]  In the United
States, it is often called Shin Buddhism.

---

[1] The literal translation of Jodo Shinshu is the True Pure Land
Religion. There are ten branches, of which the two major ones are com-
monly called Nishi Hongwanji and Higashi Honganji. Their true
names are Hompa Hongwanji and Otaniha Honganji respectively.
There are no marked doctrinal differences between these two branches; the difference is in their historical development.

[2] Shonin means "holy man."

The accepted date of the founding of the denomination is 1224 when the first draft of Shinran's most important book, *Kyo Gyo Shin Sho* (Teaching, Practice, Faith, and Attainment) was completed.

Shinran Shonin was born on May 21, 1173 in the village of Hino on the outskirts of Kyoto, Japan. When he was four years old, he lost his father, and later at the age of nine he lost his mother. Thus orphaned at an early age, the boy entered the priesthood on Mount Hiei, which was then the center of Buddhist learning.

There he was to stay for twenty years, practicing the most arduous of physical and mental disciplines. The principal teaching of the monasteries emphasized the purification of the self for the attainment of Enlightenment. Never did a young priest apply himself so wholeheartedly to all the disciplines. He soon became renowned for his scholarship and could have easily become head of one of the larger monasteries, but he was neither interested in position nor in the pursuit of knowledge. His main concern was Enlightenment. After two decades on Mount Hiei, Shinran Shonin came to the sober realization that Enlightenment was impossible for the common man. The disciplines of Mount Hiei made him acutely conscious of his own human weakness. His life was finite; his knowledge incomplete and his capacity for perfect goodness limited. Upon meditation, he discovered that in all his activities he was essentially motivated by the three poisons: greed, anger and ignorance.

In this state of mental anguish, Shinran Shonin renounced the life on Mount Hiei (see note 1). His descent from this mountain was the turning point in his religious pursuit. Shortly thereafter, he met a kindly priest, Honen, who taught a simple faith in Amida Buddha and the recitation of the Nembutsu as the way of religious fulfillment. Honen Shonin brought Shinran face to face with Amida's Infinite Wisdom and Compassion (see note 2). For the first time in his life, Shinran found inner peace in the faith that Amida Buddha was primarily concerned with such a person as he. The Buddhist life, he realized, could be lived by the man in the street without confinement to a monastery. The gate to life's meaning was now open to all, and thousands of people flocked to hear and accept the hopeful message of the Nembutsu.

The powerful monastic orders, however, feared a weakening of their long established tradition and prestige, and convinced the Imperial Court to banish Honen and Shinran, but the spiritual energy of the Nembutsu had been unleashed. The teaching soon gathered momentum as it spread from person to person and from village to village. During his years in exile, Shinran personally met with countless persons to awaken their faith in Amida Buddha.

Shinran finally settled in Inada, Japan, and then completed the first draft of *Teaching, Practice, Faith and Attainment* in 1224. In 1232, when he was fifty-nine, he returned to Kyoto. During the intervening years until his death, he wrote many books, which are read and studied even today. He died on January 16, 1262 (twenty-eighth day of eleventh month, second year of Kocho).

# Notes

(1) As long as man is quite content living an unawakened life and not knowing how to reflect on his self, he thinks that the self, existing in blind passions, is natural. However, once man searches the state of awakening and begins to reflect on himself, he will be conscious of his real nature, which can never be freed from blind passions. The more we try to negate blind passions, the more it becomes clear to us that passions are rooted in our very nature. And yet, unless these blind passions are negated, it will be impossible to realize the rational self that seeks Enlightenment. The harder we try to negate our blind passions, the more we know how difficult it is to achieve Enlightenment. The development of the rational self means the sharpening of our conscience, the deepening of realization and coming to the astonishing conclusion that our passions are unfathomably deep. As the realization of the rational self progresses, we become increasingly aware of the difficulty of eradicating passions and are faced with frustration on all sides, neither able to eradicate our blind passions nor able to find Enlightenment. This is the inner conflict Shinran Shonin experienced on Mount Hiei.

(2) The basic tenet of Shinshuology, the doctrinal organization of Jodo Shinshu, is that we are led to the realization of Buddhahood by Amida Buddha. We

cannot realize Buddhahood by ourselves, by self power, because we are tainted by the attachment to the self and all its impediments — greed, anger and ignorance (in Japanese, *bonno*). Shinran Shonin devoted twenty years of his life to approach the perfection of a Buddha and finally realized the utter futility of such an effort. At the same time, he was awakened to Amida Buddha's compassionate outreach. Only by the untainted Other Power of Amida Buddha can the ordinary person ever hope to realize Buddhahood; therefore, we must entrust ourselves to the Other Power of Amida Buddha. In short, this is the main thrust of Jodo Shinshu.

# Namo Amida Butsu
# (Recitation of the Nembutsu)

Nembutsu literally means, *I meditate on Buddha*, and Namo Amida Butsu means, *I take Refuge in Amida Buddha, the Buddha of Infinite Life and Light.*

The Nembutsu is the heart of the Buddhist religious experience. The recitation of the Nembutsu (Namo Amida Butsu), a meditation, enlightens us to our humanity and leads us to the full realization of the ultimate power of Wisdom and Compassion, which we Buddhists call Buddhahood.

Psychologically, the recitation of the Nembutsu is a conscious acceptance of Amida's Wisdom and Compassion at work. Religiously, the recitation of the Nembutsu is an act of gratitude naturally arising from an awakening to the Wisdom and Compassion of Amida Buddha. A man who lives in the supreme knowledge and profound conviction that he is now encompassed in "Amida's eternal light which never casts him away" is known as a man who lives the life of Nembutsu.

The Nembutsu is the complete identification of myself with the transcendent power of Wisdom and

Compassion from which I derive my meaning for existence. The Nembutsu is this center of my being, the spiritual home from which I operate and where I find the spiritual power to carry out all my moral, social and religious commitments. It is the verbalization of my inner awakening to the reality of life and the world. It is the sound of the Infinite touching the finite. Only in the absolute passivity of the Nembutsu do I find the unfathomable source of my life's true activity.

# Namo Amida Butsu
## (Interpretation of Characters)

The first two characters, *Namo*, mean first, to return to the original source of the universe, and secondly, to understand the meaning of Life.

*To return* has the following meaning:

To touch the heart of reality;

With great joy listen to the voice of Amida Buddha calling us;

Resting place under a gigantic tree protecting us from a terrible storm;

Amida calling us to "Rely on my protection;"

The timeless voice of Shakyamuni calling us to rely on him.

*To understand* has the following meaning:

Awaken to the real significance of Life;

Humbly accept the guiding power of Buddha;

南無阿弥陀仏

This power is the transcendent
  Other Power;
This power is always teaching us
  the truth;
It is none other than Amida guiding
  us;
All the Dharma teachers guiding
  us;
All this is the work of Amida
  Buddha;
Amida is calling us, "Come at
  once."

# Shinjin

The religious experience of Jodo Shinshu is rooted in what is known as *Shinjin* in Japanese and often defined as "the awakening of faith" in English. While the ultimate objective of life in Jodo Shinshu lies in the achievement of Buddhahood, life's immediate purpose is realized in the awakening of Faith.

There are three important components to this mind of awakening. In Japanese they are *shishin* 至心, *shingyo* 信楽, and *yokusho* 欲生, and translated respectively as: sincerity, faith, and desire for birth. Traditional Shinshu teaching says that these three minds are really one, and this one mind is bestowed upon us as a gift from Amida Buddha.

*Shishin* consists of two characters 至心. *Shi* is constructed from two ideograms: 土, which means ground, 乙 and 𠃊, which is a pictograph of a bird in flight. When the bird in flight reaches the ground we have the character shi 至. *Shin* 心 means mind. Thus when a person's true mind touches the ground of his real being, he is firmly established in his true self. He is now able to move with his whole being. There is no trace of falsehood. This is sincerity.

Let us now go to the third component, *yokusho* 欲生. This is made up of the two characters *yoku* 欲 and *sho* 生. *Yoku* has three ideograms: 𠆢, which represents the upper lip; 口, which represents mouth; and 欠, which means lacking. Thus in the character *yoku* we see a picture of a person with a faint smile on his lips, smiling at his own inadequacies. *Sho* has two parts: 土 and 丶. When these parts are combined, we have the meaning of growth as the shoots spring out from the earth. Thus *yokusho* represents a person who truly recognizes his spiritual inadequacies and aspires for spiritual growth.

*Shingyo* is made up of two characters, 信楽. The first, *shin* 信 has two parts: this radical 亻, which means a person, and this radical 言, which means words. Thus *shin* means absolute trust in a person whose word is the truth. *Gyo* 楽 has many components, 幺 and 白, which represent musical instruments or drums. The third component 木, which is the character for tree, represents a wooden stand for instruments. Here we have an orchestra complete with musical instruments and drums producing the harmonious music of the universe. When a person with his whole being, honestly realizes his spiritual inadequacies and weaknesses and seeks true spiritual growth, he will begin to hear the harmonious music of the universe. This is none other than the voice of Amida Buddha and

the great power of his Compassion, completely sur-
rounding him. He is speechless. He can only say *Namo
Amida Butsu.*

# The Pure Land

In the Jodo Shinshu school of Buddhism, the spiritual development of the person is completed with their birth in what is known as the Pure Land. (The literal translation of Jodo Shinshu is the *True Pure Land Religion*.) "Birth in the Pure Land" means the perfect growth and fulfillment of man's personality, to achieve a state of perfect selflessness whereupon one is able to realize the oneness of the whole universe; to become a Buddha and achieve Oneness with Amida Buddha. While the human weaknesses of greed, anger and ignorance are still functioning, this perfection of the personality is an impossibility.

Shinran Shonin and the teachers before him explained that the Pure Land was situated in the western corners of the universe, zillions of miles away. It was pictured as a very beautiful place, free of suffering, where everyone is happy. Philosophically speaking, however, the Pure Land does not refer to a specific location out there somewhere. Rather, the Pure Land is symbolic; it symbolizes the transcendence of relativity, of all limited qualities, of the finiteness of human life. In this transcendence, there is Compassion-Wisdom, an active moving, spiritual force. The Pure Land ideal is the culmination of the teaching of Wisdom and Compassion.

# IV

# A Life of Nembutsu

## Bodhisattva

The Bodhisattva is an aspirant to Buddhahood and ever willing to give up even his own salvation for the salvation of his fellow man. His service to his community is motivated by a deep faith in the Three Treasures: Buddha, Dharma, Sangha.[1]

---

[1] In Buddhism the Three Treasures are the Buddha, Dharma and Sangha. The Buddha is Enlightenment, the Dharma is the principle of Enlightenment and the Sangha is the assembly of people dedicated to Enlightenment. It is most significant that these are appropriately called the Three Treasures.

The supreme purpose of his life is not the pursuit of wealth and pleasure but the increase of his own virtue and wisdom as well as that of his fellow man. He therefore devotes himself to the practice of the Six Perfections: Giving, Morality, Endurance, Effort, Meditation, Wisdom.

A Bodhisattva desires all beings to develop and cultivate the following states of mind:

1. *Peace of Mind.* A Bodhisattva guides all beings toward right livelihood, far from evil living.

2. *The Mind of Ease and Comfort.* The Bodhisattva leads all beings in suffering to ease and comfort.

3. *The Mind of Compassion.* The Bodhisattva guides beings out of their hatred and brings them to good fortune.

4. *The Mind of Sorrow.* The Bodhisattva identifies himself with people in poverty and guides them out of this sad condition.

5. *The Mind of Pity and Sympathy.* The Bodhisattva leads beings out of their self-indulgence so they will never return to a life of debauchery.

6. *The Mind to Benefit Others.* The human mind always thinks of personal benefits, but the Bodhisattva's mind always thinks of guiding others to the Way of the Buddha.

7. *The Mind to Guard all Beings.* The Bodhisattva

always works to guard all fellow disciples so they will not return to their old ways.

8. *The Bodhisattva's Mind of Oneness.* This is the Mind that becomes One with all beings, transcending the dichotomy of you and me.

9. *The Mind of the Master.* The Mind of the Master is always moving and working to lead all beings to the heart of Mahayana, the Heart of Great Compassion.

We have a saying: "To destroy the lesser self and realize the Greater Self." The attainment of the Greater Self is none other than the way of the Bodhisattva. In Santideva's "Path of Light" we find the stirring words of the Bodhisattva ideal:

> *I would fain become a soother of all sorrows*
> *of all creatures. May I be a balm to the sick,*
> *a healer and servitor, until sickness come*
> *never again; may I become an unfailing store*
> *for the poor, and serve them with manifold*
> *things for their need... I would be a protector*
> *of the unprotected, a guide of wayfarers,*
> *a ship, a dyke, and a bridge for them who*
> *seek the other shore.*

We are living in a fast changing world in which our religious, ethical, social and political goals are being put to a supreme test. In such a world the high ideals of the Bodhisattva, this dynamic spirit of Compassion, must be revitalized in our daily lives so we can be of service to humankind. More than ever, understanding and enlightened persons are desperately needed in the world today.

# Chanting

Chanting is a discipline and a meditation. Two thousand five hundred years ago, the Buddha's disciples chanted in unison the lessons they had learnt from their master. In the days when writing was not universal, voicing the Dharma was a convenient method of preserving the teaching. Throughout the years this tradition has been handed down from one generation to another in all the Buddhist countries, in many languages. I have heard the chants in many countries and they have all inspired in me a reverent spirit. Another aspect to the chanting, which is very important, is that in every country to where the Buddha-Dharma had migrated, unique chants were created. Because there are now translations for all the chants, with thoughtful study we can understand the meaning and experience the feeling of each chant. Thus, in quiet contemplation we come to the heart of the Buddha-Dharma.

The following are common chants and readings heard in the services:

## Amida Kyo

This is the Smaller Sukhavati Vyuha Sutra, chanted during most memorial services. A common mistaken notion is that the chanting itself and the service bring benefits for the deceased. Jodo Shinshu entertains no such ideas. The Amida Kyo is chanted because it is a sutra extolling the virtues of Jodo (Pure Land) and Amida Buddha.

## Shoshinge

Shoshinge, or the Hymn of True Faith, was written by Shinran Shonin in which he praises Amida Buddha as well as the Seven Spiritual Fathers who showed us the way of salvation through faith in Amida.

## Junirai

Junirai, or the Twelve Hymns of Worship, were written by the first of the Seven Spiritual Fathers, Nagarjuna. It praises Amida Buddha, His Land and the Bodhisattvas.

## Sanseige or Juseige

Sanseige, or the Three Sacred Vows, is from the "Larger Sukhavati Vyuha Sutra." These vows were made by Amida while he was still a Bodhisattva. They express the deep Compassion of Amida for all.

### Sanbutsuge

Sanbutsuge, or The Praises of the Buddha, is taken from the "Larger Sukhavati Vyuha Sutra." It is a hymn sung by Hozo Bosatsu as he was about to make the forty-eight vows before the Buddha — *Sejizaio Butsu.*

### Psalms of Shinran Shonin

These psalms were written in praise of Amida Buddha, His Ojodo, His Name, Namo Amida Butsu, and urges his fellow beings to place their Faith in Amida.

### Dialogues of Rennyo

Rennyo Shonin, the ninth descendant of Shinran Shonin, was a great reformer who is often spoken of as the master who actually organized the Jodo Shinshu Church. These short sayings are on a variety of subjects and are truly good advice for the ordinary layman.

### Epistles

Epistles, or *Gobunsho*, are letters written by Rennyo Shonin to followers living in outlying districts. These letters were written for various occasions such as to inspire those who were in despair after the loss of a loved one, or as instructions to priests. The letters always urged all to place their faith in Amida and to recite the Nembutsu with a grateful heart.

# Meditation

Meditation is a spiritual discipline that deepens and expands our awareness. In the practice of meditation, one tranquilizes the mind to be like the mind of the Buddha — calm, peaceful and undisturbed. The tranquility of the mind is the first step towards understanding the heart of reality, to see the true nature of the universe. Just as the stars of the night sky are reflected on the surface of a calm lake, so is the truth of the self reflected on the tranquil mind.

Individual meditation gives us the opportunity for self-reflection and penetrating insight into our existential being — into the murky depths of our own being — with all its selfishness, passions and ignorance. Such reflection brings us face to face with our inner self and the possible motives for our actions, thus leading us to honestly ask ourselves, "Is the motive for my actions greed, hatred, anger, jealousy or ignorance?"

While the mind is restless with the incessant waves of *bonno* — the human passions of greed, anger and ignorance — the truth of the self can never be mirrored on the mind. For in greed, our minds repel all thoughts of the needs of others. In anger, our minds lose all sense of reason and balance. In ignorance, our minds become myopic.

From the story of the Buddha:

*After Gautama had accepted a bowl of rice gruel from the village maiden, Sujata, he sat quietly under the Bodhi Tree. There he vowed that he would never move until he had attained Enlightenment. Then King Mara sent his army of one hundred million eight thousand demons who fired their crossbows and brandished their swords. Heaven and earth were enveloped in darkness and the sound of thunder was terrifying. Evil demons and yakkas and their cohorts, all with grotesque appearances, all with heads of lions, bears, cows and horses spewed forth flames of poison, rained down all kinds of weapons. Ugly temptations rose in the Prince's mind. But he remained steadfast in his resolve to attain Enlightenment. In this way, the Prince, who, in one day reached the summit of his crisis, attained tranquility of mind and entered into a meditative state.*

In meditation he, who with a tranquil mind sees the huge army of Mara attacking from all directions, is unafraid, for he realizes that the general in command of this vast army is none other than himself. He need only to issue the command, "Halt!"

# Meditation Sutra on Infinite Life

The educational methods used by the Buddha for personal awakening should be studied by modern followers of the Buddha. These methods are enunciated in the *Meditation Sutra on Infinite Life*, sometimes called *The Tragedy of Rajagrha*. This sutra describes the mental anguish of a once powerful queen, Vaidehi, who is imprisoned by her own son, Prince Ajatasatru. In her dark cell she is filled with self-pity and self-righteousness. The Buddha realizes that this unconscious spiritual imprisonment is a far greater problem than her physical imprisonment. Vaidehi has built an impenetrable wall of blind self-attachment around her, having nothing but hate for her son, his followers, even the Buddha and the entire world. The Buddha talks to her gently and guides her to meditate on the setting sun, the beauty of the waters, the land, the trees, the lakes, the Bodhisattvas, and other indescribably beautiful objects. In this manner the steel gate of her own mental prison gradually opens and lets in the Light of Wisdom.

The Buddha teaches Vaidehi that the Infinite Light of Amida Buddha permeates all things in the universe, even her dark mind. In one of the most startling lines in the sutra the Buddha says to her, "It is this mind that becomes Buddha; indeed it is this mind that is Buddha." Vaidehi is suddenly awakened from her dream and is now able to follow the Buddha humbly to deeper insight.

# The Essential Meaning of
the Meditation Sutra

The *Essential Meaning of the Meditation Sutra* is a commentary on the *Kanmuryojukyo* by Shan-tao[1] and begins with the verses which might be called, "The Gatha of Utmost Reverence." The following is a free translation of this gatha. To those who practice the Way of the Buddha, it inspires them to exert even greater effort to realize the Way. Because of its lofty religious aspiration it is chanted at funeral services to comfort and give strength to the family members, especially in their hour of deep grief.

Firstly, I urge you all to awaken your Bodhi mind
and take refuge in the Three Treasures.

Priests and laymen of the present day,
awaken your Bodhi mind,
you, who find great difficulty in escaping
the delusion of birth and death and know not how to
rejoice in the Buddha-Dharma.

---

[1] Shan-tao (613-681). One of seven masters in the line of transmission of the teaching of the Jodo Shinshu sect of Pure Land Buddhism.

Awaken your Bodhi mind to Amida's
Compassion and leap across the swift currents
of birth, old age, sickness and death
and enter Amida's Pure Land.
With Gassho and Respect
show reverence to Amida Buddha.

O Blessed One, with one mind and heart
I take refuge in you and in all
the Buddhas of the universe
who emerge from the Sea of Enlightenment;
who appear in the lower world of beings
to lead all to Buddhahood with every
skilled means.

The great assembly of Bodhisattvas —
all are free of bonno, free from even a taint
of greed, anger and ignorance.
They all have perfected their disciplines
and have gained wisdom, insight and freedom —
the attainment of the incomparable
Enlightenment.

You, who suffer in delusion,
receive the diamond faith of awakening,
and following the Buddha's Way,
take refuge in the Buddha and
the Bodhisattvas.

We shall take refuge in these great Teachers
whose ultimate concern is the Enlightenment
of all beings.
May they bestow their enlightening
power on all of us.

We shall receive the Buddha's great Mind
of Compassion and never falter in our efforts.
May the Buddha guide us always in our
humble efforts.
In each thought we shall be mindful
of the Buddha.

We are foolish beings
who have wandered in delusion from
time immemorial.
Now in this decadent age, hundreds of years
after Buddha's Nirvana,
how fortunate we are to meet Amida's Primal
Vow that leads us straight to Peace and Bliss.

I direct my Bodhisattva thoughts and practices
to Buddhahood and becoming one with Amida
Buddha, compose this verse to take refuge
in the Buddha, Dharma and Sangha.
May the Buddhas of the ten directions,
numbering more than the sands of the Ganges,
awaken our darkest minds with their
inconceivable power of Compassion.

I take refuge in the Teaching of Sakyamuni and
Amida Buddha
and open wide the gate for all beings
so that they may enter the pure Realm of
Enlightenment.

May the gifts bestowed upon me by Amida Buddha,
be equally shared with all beings
and together, awakening our Bodhi mind,
realize the Perfect Realm of Peace and Bliss.

*84,000 Thoughts*

The meditations on the following pages originally appeared in the column, "84,000 Thoughts," in the publications *Kalavinka,* and *Wheel of Dharma.*

# Naturalness

I once saw the moon rising from the Alberta prairies, a huge bright orange ball, the biggest moon I had ever seen. I used to think the desert was one monotonous stretch of sand, but when I visited Arizona I saw the primordial beauty of the desert in the sunset, the Saguaro cactus, standing like a sentinel guarding the unspoiled domain.

Beauty in naturalness abounds everywhere, the quiet forests, the pounding sea, the laughter of children, the silent dignity of sorrow....

Here in Virginia, in the hot humid evenings the fireflies light up the lawns with their natural glow and the cicadas join the myriad of insects in the recitation of the Nembutsu.

# Fireflies

From ancient times we humans have always been fascinated by these little beings. Scientists explain that the firefly's light is produced through a complicated interaction of a number of chemicals. But for me, its light teaches a very valuable lesson: the firefly is not poisonous and does not bite; its lifespan is short and in its brief moments on earth, *it just gives off light.*

I believe the light it emanates is truly its Buddha-nature.

As for me, I am stronger, more intelligent, civilized and live longer, but I cannot give light. It makes me very humble.

# August 27, 1981

It is that time of the year. A single red maple leaf performs a graceful ballet in the cool autumn breeze before it finally joins the other leaves on the ground. During the warm spring days and in the hot summer heat, it gave shelter to countless insects, even giving a part of itself to the hungry bugs.

And now, it is that time of the year. But before it falls from its branch, it prepares for the future, for next spring a fresh green leaf will shoot out from the same branch. In its twilight hours it displayed to the world, without pride, without self-consciousness, its ultimate beauty.

Does the human spirit grow more beautiful with each passing day? Or does it become more engrossed in its mortality by creating stronger hands of self-attachment.

Is my life reflecting a deeper beauty as I grow older? What karmic influences will I leave for the good of the world?

I wonder. In the quiet of the night, I recite the Nembutsu.

# Listen

Listen. Listen to the voice of the Dharma.
Listen to the birds, singing in the morning,
the wind sighing in the boughs overhead,
and the roar of the waves on the beach.

Listen to the rain on the roof and the snow falling in the fields.

The Dharma speaks to us through the sounds of the world —
forcefully and eloquently and beautifully.
It speaks of the unending change around us,
the immutable truth of interdependence,
and the peace in nature.
Do we have the ears to hear and listen...?

Listen to the Nembutsu in the Hondo.
Listen to the noble silence of the Buddha.

# Cosmic Energy

A distant star, shining for aeons of time in the darkness of space, one cosmic day explodes and becomes a swirling mass of gas. This mass unites with other gases in some distant future and gives birth to another extraterrestrial body. This unending process is cosmic energy, which changes from one form to another but is never dissipated.

A blade of grass at my feet turns brown with the changing seasons and withers away in the cold night. But in a real sense it never dies, for the roots nurtured in the rich soil produce another blade one spring morning. This blade is different from its immediate ancestor but similar in many respects because the source of its life is the powerful life giving energy of its spindly but tenuous roots.

The life that pulsates in me is changing every moment — birth, old age, sickness and death — and birth again to repeat the endless cycle.

We call this energy the Infinite Light and Life of the Universe. The Buddhist way of life is not to fight the currents and rapids of life but to move in harmony with the eternal flow of cosmic energy. This is the life of Nembutsu. Shinran said, *"I place my mind in the soil of Buddha's Universal Vow and let my thoughts flow into the sea of the inconceivable Dharma."*

My life energy, which I selfishly call my own, is really a cosmic energy. I do not own it; it belongs to the universe. While it operates in me, I must realize that I must direct it towards compassionate ends.

# Oso Eko, Genso Eko[1]

The waters of the river all flow on to reach the wide expanse of the sea. In time the water evaporates and becomes clouds and when cumulus clouds are saturated with moisture, it is released to return to the surface of the earth as rain. The raindrops that fall from the skies sustain the life of all living things from the tallest redwoods to the tiniest insects that crawl on the ground.

I believe that this cycle is analogous to the dynamic cycle of human life. When the body is buried in the ground it becomes the soil in which other living things grow. When the body is cremated, the smoke rises to the heavens and the molecules of gas enter the atmosphere which all living things breathe. We humans are so attached to the body we think that death is the absolute end. Death is only the dissolution of the physical body; death is the end of the physical existence but

---

[1] In Japanese the water flowing to the sea may be called *oso eko*, or the going phase of the movement; the raindrops falling on the earth may be called *genso eko*, or the return to the place of origin.

not the end of life. In reality it is the beginning of a great interaction with the universe.

Further, human life is more than physical energy; it is moral and spiritual energy. Released upon the world, this influence continues to operate throughout the universe. How many times have we read the words of the Buddha and other masters and found an unending source of inspiration, comfort, strength, and a practical guide to living. How many times have you picked up an old letter written by your long departed mother or father, wife or husband and quietly contemplated its contents. That person's karmic energies or the person's Dharma — their visions, dreams, activities, words and thoughts — will continue to exert their powerful influence on the minds and hearts of those who knew them.

Every human life is a source of the energy of compassion stored in the depth of its innate Buddhahood. It may be but a microscopic part of the Cosmic Compassion of the Universe, which religiously we call *Amida Buddha*, but once the part becomes immersed in the Cosmic Compassion, it flows in harmony with its mighty current. Just as the waters of the river return from the depth of the ocean to quench the thirsty surface of our planet, so does human energy, now purified in Buddhahood, return to this world to continue its perpetual work of compassion.

# Eternal Now

In the beginningless, endless flow of time
each life is a mere ripple,
existing only for an instantaneous moment
and disappearing forever.

But each life is a unique experience
with beauty and truth, all of its own
with no identical counterpart in history
and none absolutely the same in the future.

Your life, my life —
is attuned to the rhythm of the cosmos
and to the heartbeat of reality.

Each life exists in the Eternal Now.

Each idea that is thought,
each word that is spoken,
each action that is taken,
changes the whole pattern of the universe
for the universe is interdependent.
Think, speak and act, then,
always in the eternal now

with compassion and understanding
for your own enlightenment
and for the enlightenment of all sentient beings.

# Namo Amida Butsu

The Nembutsu is the sound of the universe.
It is the sound of the wind
as it rustles the leaves;
It is the roar of the waves
as they rush toward the shore;
It is the song of the robin, the whippoorwill
and the chorus of cicadas on a summer evening.
The Nembutsu is naturalness...
The first cry of the baby
as it emerges into the world
from the darkness of the mother's womb;
It is the powerful cry of independence
of individuality, of selfhood;
But it is also the great cry of awakening
to its dependence on something greater than self...
for its sustenance.
The Nembutsu is the proclamation of the Buddha...
"Above heaven and below heaven, I alone am the
World Honored One."
It is the ultimate declaration of life;
I alone hold my destiny in my hand
leading to perfect Buddhahood.
When I touch the heart of reality,

It is Namo Amida Butsu...
What else can I say?
When I truly share someone's happiness,
it is Namo Amida Butsu;
And in that moment of deep grief
over a loved one's death,
it is just Namo Amida Butsu.
Namo Amida Butsu...
it is the song of gratitude
not of my finding the Buddha,
but Buddha finding me.

My life is fleeting and finite and I do not know with certitude what tomorrow has in store for me. But in the transitory boundaries of my existence is the timeless flow of Amida's life. In the finite sound of my Nembutsu is Amida's voice of Compassion, tirelessly calling me. Like a small stream that enters the mighty current of the great river, so does my insignificant life, in the Nembutsu, join the majestic flow of Amida's Infinite Life.
*Namo Amida Butsu.*

k.t.t.